I0438035

THOUGH THE SCARS ARE GREAT, JESUS IS THE GREAT HEALER

Isaiah 1:18

by

Lekeshia Bonner

authorHOUSE®

AuthorHouse™
1663 Liberty Drive, Suite 200
Bloomington, IN 47403
www.authorhouse.com
Phone: 1-800-839-8640

© 2009 Lekeshia Bonner. All rights reserved.

No part of this book may be reproduced, stored in a retrieval system, or transmitted by any means without the written permission of the author.

First published by AuthorHouse 2/4/2009

ISBN: 978-1-4343-7041-9 (sc)

Printed in the United States of America
Bloomington, Indiana

This book is printed on acid-free paper.

Scriptures taken from King James Version and New Living Translation.

Dedication

I would like to give all thanks and glory to God for all He has done in my life, And I thank God for trusting me with His word.

I give honor to my wonderful and awesome loving husband, Bradley, who put up with me through many trials and tribulations, and who loved me through all of my faults. I just want you to know I love you, and I thank God for you, knowing that He gave me a man of God after His own heart.

To my four beautiful, loving, and adorable kids; Jarvaris, Tanquile, J'Quan, and Joshua: Mama loves her babies.

To my mother, Barbara, and father, George, I love you both, and I thank God for you being my parents. It took me some time to realize you are the parents God meant for me to have. I am grateful, and once again I love you both dearly.

To my sisters and brothers; Alicia, Carolyn, Teresa, Tamekia, Michael, Jeffery, Melvin, Torris, Arthur, and Frederick; I love you all from the bottom of my heart.

To my nieces and nephews, I love you all, and remember: you are all my babies.

To my Pastors, Deloise and Elton Johnson, I thank God for you each and every day. Pastor Deloise, I thank you for your love and support and for you being such an inspiration in my life. I am very grateful to have you in my life. You have been there for me through some of the hardest trials in my life more than you will ever know. Pastor Elton, I thank God for the courage you gave me. I remember when I was a little discouraged in the midst of writing this book; God would allow you to ask me "how is the book coming?" Thank you for the courage you gave me so I did not abort this book, but allowed it to come forth. I just want to say thank you, and I love you both.

Also I would like to say to my church family at the House Of Praise Church Of The Living God, I love you and thank God for you because we have been taught to love, support, and be there for one another, knowing that if we hurt our brother or sister we only hurt ourselves. In unity we stand, and divided we fall.

To my mother-in-law and father-in-law, Deacon Ardie and Annie, Grandma Rosia, my sister-in-law and brother-in-law, Shanika and Norris, and my two nieces-in-law. I love each of you. I thank God for your big, loving hearts.

Introduction

I was inspired by God to write this book to let others (the broken-hearted, rejected, lost, hurting, and wounded souls) know, regardless of what circumstances or situations they are faced with, God is able to deliver them and bring them through every test, trial, and tribulation. This book was written not to harm anyone, but only to let others know that God is a restorer, healer and deliverer. He loves his people, and they are on His mind.

Chapter One:
The God Who Heals Broken Hearts and Heals Emotions

As I look back over my life and think about all the things He (Jesus) has brought me out of and how I overcame the devil, I know how much Jesus loves me. One of the main things the Lord brought me out of was fornication, which is one of the biggest sins that's going on in the world today. (Let me remind you; God said in his word that no sin is greater than the others. All sin stinks in the nostrils of God. He forgives the individual and loves the person, but He hates the sin.)

People don't realize what Satan has set up for them, and it is affecting them spiritually and emotionally. I have learned a good lesson from my mistakes, and I don't want anyone else to go through what I have gone through.

When I was a little girl, my father was not in my life like he should have been. All I wanted was my father and mother to take me in their arms and tell me they loved me and were proud of me. I tried to find love in other people, but I have come to realize that I can't find love in other people that will fill the void of not having the love of a father or mother I though I should have gotten when I was a child. Only Jesus can love you in that area of your life.

One day as I was seeking God, He allowed me to see my parents' hearts. You see, the same thing happened to my parents, so because of their own hurt, wounds, and scars, they didn't allow God to heal their hearts. This is what stopped them from throwing their arms around me and telling me they loved me and were proud of me. It was not intended, because even they were unaware of it. And God spoke to me and said, "Daughter, forgive and forget about the past and embrace what I am doing now in your life and your parents' life. Accept the love they give to you now." So each and every day I thank God for my parents. Mom and Dad, I love you dearly.

If you are experiencing this emotional pain, I encourage you to push past your hurt and allow God to heal your broken heart. (He wants to heal your heart, mind, body, and soul.) What greater love do we have than Jesus? None.

You see, it was love that kept Jesus up on the cross He had the power to call out to His Father, and God would have sent twelve legions of Angels from heaven, but because of the love

He has for us, He stayed right there. "Thinkest thou that I cannot now pray to my Father, and He shall presently give me more than twelve legions of Angels?" Matt. 26:53

No matter what the hurt is, it might not have come from a childhood; it may be from a bad relationship, or it may be that someone has let you down and it broke your heart or disappointed you in life. It all is just still hurt, and God wants to heal your heart, but you must allow him to do so. When you make up your mind that you are going to push past the pain and allow God to go to the root of the problem and go deep down into the innermost part of your heart, where you have been hurt, God will heal your heart, and you will be able to forgive and love the person without seeing the hurt that they have caused you. "He heals the broken hearted and binds up their wounds." Ps. 147:3

All I wanted was for someone to love me. I began to look for love in all the wrong places. I started drinking, going out to nightclubs, smoking pot (marijuana), and having sex, and I began to think to myself *If I have a baby, I will have someone to love me and not leave me.* (This was just a trick of the enemy.) So one day I met a guy who was six years older than me, but he didn't know it at the time because I lied about my age, and he didn't find out the truth about my age until I was pregnant. As we began to date, we became friends, and we began to go steady with one another. I though I was in love, but I was only kidding myself because I didn't love myself, and I didn't know how to love anyone else until I allowed God to come into my life and teach me how to love Him (God) first and myself second, and now I can love someone else. The guy didn't know how to love me, either, because he had been wounded and hurt during his childhood. He had scars and pain from his childhood as well. When he was about fourteen years old, his mother died, and his Father wasn't there for him, so as you can see, we were just two hurting people that connected and tried to make each other complete. However, only Jesus could have made us complete. You can only find completeness in Jesus. (Acts 9:34)

I want to warn every teenager: if you are contemplating that if you have a child you will have someone to love you, or if you are thinking, *I will have a baby to hold on to a man,* It won't work. You just need to know in your heart that you are loved. And you may even think your parents don't love you (that's a lie from the enemy). Your parents do love you. Jesus loves you no matter what you do or what you have done. He loves you with an everlasting love(Jer. 31:3), and it is unconditional, which means you don't have to do anything to try to make Him (Jesus) love you, because He already does. And no one can love us like He (Jesus) does. "Herein is love, not that we loved God, but that He loved us, and sent his son to be the propitiation for our sins." John 4:10

God loved us so much that He expressed his love by sending His only begotten son (Jesus) to die for the sins of the world (John 3:16). In reality you have to give a child love; you can't expect the child to love you, because you have to nurture that child and impart love in the child. Then the child will be able to love you, because you will have imparted love in the child.

If you have an empty and void feeling that makes you think you need something or someone to love you, allow God to touch you in those areas in your life in which you can experience his unconditional love.

seek counselor?

"there is safety in the multitude of counselors." Prov. 11:14

By seeking godly counsel, you can save yourself a lot of heartache and pain. If you don't reach out for help, you might just fall into Satan's trap, because truly it is only a trap that the enemy has set up for you. Reaching out may prevent you from having to raise a child by yourself, young ladies, because 75 percent of the average mens today will be a man and take care of their children (this is not a fact, but an opinion).

Children needs a mother and father to be there to give them the nuture, love, and support they need. There are some areas a mother can not fill in a child, because it is designed by God for the father to fill them, and there are some areas a Father cannot fill, because those areas are designed by God for the mother to fill.

Yes, you can raise a child by yourself, but that child may feel like he or she has missed that father or mother part of his or her life. Besides, God never intended for us to raise children as single parents. (I'm not trying to insult anyone, because I was a single parent for years.) God's will is for husbands and wives to have children to replenish the earth. Sex is for married people, because God told us in his word "Be Ye Holy for I am Holy." Lev. 11:45

Your body is the temple of the Holy Ghost (1Cor. 6:19). Come to realize that you are not only hurting yourself, but that you are also destroying the temple of the Holy Ghost. But thank God for Jesus.

If you have had children out of wed lock.

He is a forgiving God, and He still loves you. If this has happened to you, don't beat yourself up, because God loves you and He forgives you, even though I had children before I was married, it was done out of the will of God. You see, the young man and I planned to have a child. I thought he loved me and would never leave me, but sadly, I was a naive teenager.

Reflections and Thoughts

Reflections and Thoughts

Reflections and Thoughts

Chapter Two:
God's Unconditional Love

A few weeks after I gave birth to our son, I found out the father was cheating on me. I was so hurt I couldn't believe it. And I was ashamed, I remember seeing people look at me strangely while I was walking down the street. Even my family was looking at me funny; they knew what had happened, but they really didn't know the pain I was going through on the inside.

People would say to me, "What's wrong? You look like you lost your best friend." I began to hide all of my pain on the inside. I told myself I wasn't going to cry. I was depressed and miserable. He denied it to the end, but on the inside I knew it was true. I just didn't want to accept that it was true. I was living with my mom at the time, so I went and got my own house. I didn't want anyone to see me cry myself to sleep at night, and I thought if we lived together it would change things. It never did. Instead of getting better, it became worse. One day I told him I wanted to be married. He brought me an engagement ring, but in his heart, he was not ready to be married. We never set a date for the wedding. The more I tried to please him, the harder the situation got. But as I look back at the situation, I know that he was not the husband God had chosen for me, and God was not pleased with me living with this man, because our living together while not being married was a sin and it was wrong.

I have learned this is one reason God said people should not have sex before marriage. I should have waited until God sent me a husband in the first place. People, please wait until God sends you the husband or wife that he intends for you to have.

The relationship went from there being another woman to him abusing me. I was not saved, and I didn't know God at that time. But on the inside, I wanted more out of life, and I remember the times I used to say to God, "It hurts so bad; stop my heart from hurting like this."

It became so bad that we began to sleep in separate bedrooms. I tried to put him out, but I didn't have the will power to ask him to leave, because I was afraid of being alone. There were times he would come in my room or I would go in his room and he would have sex with me, and I thought that if I allowed him to do this, he would love me, and I even thought he would know that I loved him (a trick of Satan).

You don't have to have sex with someone to prove you love them. Just know that God loves you.

Afterward he went on about his business, still doing what he wanted to do. I felt very hurt, lost, and rejected, and I had no one to talk to. I began to try to lose weight (I was only 175 pounds), thinking he would love me, but it still didn't work. And it was not going to work, because it was sin and God can't bless sin. I found out only God could love me in those broken places in my life. You have got to know that if you didn't have a father or mother figure in your life or that if someone has hurt, wounded, abused, or rejected you, only God can heal that part of you, because that is a part of your life God has reserved for himself, and himself only.

If you desire to date someone, God will allow you to if it is in his standards and as long as you keep God first and the head of it all. Anytime you have sex before you are married it means that you have not put God first and that He is not the center of the relationship.

In the midst of all of my depression and wanting my heart to stop aching, the devil placed someone else in my life. This was a big mistake. Don't ever use one bad relationship to get over another bad relationship; it only adds hurt on top of hurt. Allow your heart to be healed by God. I should have ran to the altar and found Jesus, but sadly I didn't know how, and there was no one in my life to teach me how. So I ended up getting out of one bad relationship and going straight into another bad relationship. Big mistake. Once again, never allow yourself to jump out of one relationship into another. Please allow God to heal your heart. Don't take old baggage and mix it with new baggage, because when you have a small disagreement in the current relationship, you will begin to deal with hurt from the old relationship as well as that of the present relationship. This will lead to hurt on top of hurt.

Reflections and Thoughts

Reflections and Thoughts

Chapter Three:
Give Up the Baggae

At first I did not want to get involved. I was so lonely, and I just wanted someone to talk to. The pain was so great; I just wanted someone to love me. One night while I was in the car with my sister, this guy came over and asked my sister to introduce me to him. My sister was dating his friend at the time. Unfortunately, I did not know at the time that this was the beginning of an even bigger heartache. We began to meet up and talk. In the process, he told me he was just coming out of a bad relationship. I found out it was a lie. Even though he lied to me, I continued seeing him because he listened to me and pretend to be concerned about me. He made me feel special and treated me with respect. At first, I fell in love with him. He seemed to be all that I was looking for. He would not curse around me. He was polite even if we had an argument he would not call me names. He would talk to me for hours. He even started sharing some things about his hurtful past with me. There was a bond that grew stonger between us. I thought I had met Prince Charming. This was another trick from Satan; one day the devil jumped out of the box. Little did I know I was only on my way to more heartache and pain. The only difference between this relationship and the past one was that there was no physical abuse in this one. We had arguments about other women, the verbal abuse was worse, and I had such low self-esteem that I even accepted him living with another woman until one day I got tired of him coming over to my house, having sex with me, and leaving to go home with her. It would leave me feeling hurt, lonely, rejected, and most of all, confused.

I thank God for delivering me. That was a very painful time in my life. There were times when I didn't think I was going to make it because the pain was so great.

If it wasn't for Jesus, I probably would be in a crazy house. Let me explain why I say this: I used to lie in my bed at night and just cry myself to sleep. My heart was heavy, and I was depressed. I used to walk around with a smile on my face while on the inside I was hurting and miserable. I began to drink more heavily and smoke cigarettes. I had no one to talk to and nowhere to turn.

I used to always say people knew what they are doing when they were drunk, but I found out you can get so drunk that you can have blackouts. I got very drunk. We got into and argument, and I was trying to make him talk to me. I remember making a U-turn in the middle of a main street and following him home. He began to close the door. I pushed the door open, and he pushed me in my chest, shoving me back out the door. I was dumb-founded. I was thinking, *Why is he acting like this?* I didn't understand, so I went out to my car and pulled a hammer out from underneath my seat and began to smash his car windows. He came running outside. I looked up and saw him running toward me, so I ran and jumped back into my car. I must have gone to sleep; it was like I had a blackout, because I can't tell you what happened for the next twenty minutes. I remember him throwing bricks and bottles at my car, and two of my tires were flat one on the passenger's side and one on the driver's side. The next thing I remember is getting out of my car; I had to throw my window on the ground because it was in my lap.

I had to hold my hands up in the air while the police handcuffed me, and then they took me off to jail. Later on the young man told me that the police had pulled their guns on me. I had to stay in jail for seven hours. I slept the whole six hours and thirty minutes. When I woke up, I thought I was dreaming, only to find out it wasn't a dream and I was in jail. As I began to rub my hands together, I could feel glass in the tips of my fingers. I remember the bailer saying to me, "You slept like a baby. You have thirty more minutes, but I am going to let you go." I was charged with disorderly conduct, but I thank God for sparing my life, because if that brick the young man threw through the driver's side window had hit me in the head, I could have suffered brain damage or been killed, and sadly to say, if I had died in that state of sin, I would have opened my eyes in hell.

So that's why I am so grateful to God and I praise him for looking beyond all of my faults. Jesus saw my needs, and He knew that I needed to be saved.

There were times when I felt like I couldn't go on, but something on the inside of me just wouldn't let me give up. So I began to ask Him to make a choice, and He said he didn't know how; He couldn't just jump up and leave this woman, because they had been together several years and he didn't want to live in another city. Because of my previous relationship, I had made up my mind that I was not going to live with another man unless I was married to him.

He told me he didn't love her and that if he ever was to get married, I would be the one he would marry. As I look at it now, I realize that he probably was telling her the same thing. It was just a lie to keep me from walking away. But sadly, I did believe him at the time, so I thought to myself, *If he ain't going to leave her, I might as well let her know about me.* So one day he left home like he was going to work and he spent the day over at my house, and when he left I called her and told her about our relationship. He was angry, but he still didn't stop seeing me. You see, I had money, a car that was paid for, nice clothes, and jewelry, but I was miserable and empty on the inside. So I thought to myself, *If I have a baby by him then he will be with me and want to raise his first child.* (I thought it was his first child. He had told me about a child that was possible his child. But in my mind, I blocked all of that out.) So I stopped taking my birth control shots. I thought that a child by him would be something she wasn't able to give him. And this would be a reason for him to love me. I could have given him a child (another trick from the enemy). You see, I found out the hard way. I don't care how many children you have for a man; if he don't love you, it is not going to make him love you, and it sure won't make him do right in being with you. Having children for a man is not going to change his heart; only God can. I came to the conclusion that I didn't want anyone to love me out of force, but I wanted someone who would love me out of a free will and heart.

I am reminded of the passage in Gen. 30–35 (New Living Translation):

"So Jacob slept with Rachel, too, and he loved her more than Leah. He stayed and worked the additional seven years. But because Leah was unloved, the Lord let her have a child, While Rachel was childless. So Leah became pregnant and had a son. She named Reuben, for she said, the Lord has noticed my misery, and now my husband will love me. She soon became pregnant again and had another son. She named him Simeon, for she said "the Lord heard that I was unloved and he has given me another son."Again she became pregnant and had a son. She named him Levi, and she said, "Surely now my husband will feel affection for me, Since I have given him three sons." Once again she became pregnant and had a son. She named him Judah, for she said "Now I will praise the Lord." And then she stopped having children.

As you can see, in spite of Leah kept having baby after baby, thinking that her husband (Jacob) would love her, the truth of the matter was that Jacob loved Rachel and favored her over Leah, and the children Leah kept having didn't change the love he had for her. So I tried to get pregnant for two years straight, and I just couldn't get pregnant. One day I went to a therapist's office. I began to tell the therapist about all the problems I was having. He looked at me and He pulled a pamphlet out explaining how to accept Jesus as your Lord and personal Savior. I felt even worse. I didn't understand, and I felt even more lost and confused because he gave me the pamphlet and he told me to pray every night before going to sleep, but he didn't explain it to me. One night when I was at home, I was so depressed. I cried constantly. While at my lowest point, satan started talking to me. He even had me thinking about committing suicide. I thought long and hard about doing it, but God had other plans. As I began to study the word of God, I realized that suicide is just a short trip to hell. I thank God for His mercy and His grace. And I thank Him for keeping me even when I was a wretch undone. He kept me even when I did not know Jesus in the parting of my sins. God loved me, and he kept his loving arms around me. I had a bottle of alcohol and a bottle of pills on the back of the toilet in my bathroom. Like I told you earlier, I was dealing with old baggage as well as the present baggage. My doorbell rang. My ex-boyfriend had come over and wanted to talk to me about getting back together. He asked if he could use the bathroom. I forgot about the pills and alcohol being in the bathroom. I remember him coming out of the bathroom; he was very afraid because he thought I had taken the pills and the alcohol. I remember him saying to me, "Kesha, I love you." He just held me in his arms and talked to me all night, and I don't even remember dozing off to sleep. But that's one of the reasons he always had a special place in my heart. I would have done anything to help him, and I thank God for using him to spare my life. It was God that spared my life; God just used him as a vessel by sending him over that night at the right time.

Reflections and Thoughts

Reflections and Thoughts

Chapter Four:
The God Who Delivers

I was invited to come to church by a friend in another city. We thought we could party and do what we wanted to and it was all right (a trick from the enemy). It wasn't a spirit-filled church, but I was sitting in that church thinking, *God I just want more of you.* I had visited a spirit-filled church about two times in the city where I lived.

At the time I visited the spirit-filled church, I just felt like I was ready, for more but that Sunday morning, while I was sitting in my friend's church, on the inside I felt myself wanting to say *"Thank you, Jesus, and praise God."* Weeks went by, and one Sunday morning I was at home, getting dressed to go back out of town to go to a club party on a Sunday evening, but suddenly the telephone rang, and it was a friend that attended a spirit-filled church I had visited before in the city in which I lived. It was not normal for her to call me on a Sunday morning, and it was not by chance she caught me at home, because I really had stopped staying at home. She said, "Get up; you have to go to some church." Now, she said more than just that. I know she had no way of knowing, I had not told her the things she told me. There was something on the inside of me that was afraid. I knew I had to go to church somewhere, because I was afraid something bad would have happen to me if I didn't go. So I visited her church that Sunday morning. The word of God convicted my heart to accept Jesus Christ as my Lord and Savior that Sunday morning. And I found myself just continually going back to that church. I just couldn't get enough of the word. And the people made me feel very loved, even though some members had attitudes because they didn't want anyone to get closer to the pastor than themselves, but I didn't let that stop me, because I knew God had place me in that church. I had gone to other churches, but I couldn't relate to the word in them like I did in this one. At first I thought I could have kept doing what I wanted to do. But I had only back slidden. I wanted to keep my sugar daddy and still continue to go to church thinking I could still feel the anointing of God, but I was wrong. The only thing I was doing was setting myself back, making it seven times harder to get out of fornication than it already was. I began to start backing away little by little from church until I had an accident one night. I was supposed to go to church, but one of my old girlfriends kept calling me to ask me to come to her house. They had a full house and alcohol. I allowed the devil to have a very big strong hold on my life; he had me bound. In order to get free, sometimes it takes surrounding yourself with the saints of God (Luke 22:32). God gave me a godmother who later on became my pastor. She began to talk to me and tell me that fornication was wrong and was not pleasing to God. So I began hanging around her. I wanted to live the holy life that I saw her living. I wanted to do right, but I just couldn't stop going back to fornication (because I didn't have the keeper: the Holy Ghost). I would tell myself, "Well, I'll just do it one last time, but that one last time turned into another one and another, and I found out I was pregnant, and then I really found out how much he really loved me. Deep down on the inside I knew he was not in love with me, but I wanted to make myself believe differently. Through all of this, I was hearing my pastor preaching the word of God, saying to the church, "If you don't come out of your sin, in hell you will lift your eyes," and my godmother was telling me the same thing on the other side. That left me only one choice: shape up or ship out. I started to want the things of God for my life. I always did want those things; I just wanted to keep my sugar daddy, too. I was willing to marry him and then let God change him. I was willing to accept him just like he was. But it was not in the word of God, and that was not the will of God for my life. And it seemed like every time God would deliver me and I would go back to the same situation, until one day, when God opened my eyes. As I look back over my life and I think about all the things God has brought me out of, it lets me know how much God really loves me. I knew my pastor and godmother got tired of me always running to them with my problems, but being the loving people they were, they just continued to encourage and love me. I know it was the love of God that caused them to put up with me, because I was tired of myself. I'm just glad they didn't give up on me. I was pregnant and heartbroken. I made up my mind that I would never love another person to the pointed that I would allow them to come between me and God. While I was pregnant, I still continued to see him, thinking that I could change him, even though I knew how he felt about my pregnancy. You see, he wanted me to have an abortion. I told myself that he was only playing and that he loved me. I made myself believe he was excited because this was his first child, but I was wrong once more. One night we had a big argument, and something on the inside told me that the things he said to me were his true feelings, and I still stayed with him. I felt like I was not strong enough to let go. So I continued to stay with him, but all the time my feelings for him were changing day by day. You see, that night when he said what he said, something on the inside of me just wanted to leave him, but I couldn't, because he was a soul tie. I felt like I was in a web, wanting to get out but not able to (Matt.12:45) tells us if God delivers us from a spirit and we go back to it, the spirit come back with seven more spirits. Not only that, but it is harder to come out of our sins the second time than it was the first time. I knew in my heart I needed to let go. One day my pastor was preaching, and he said, "If you give up boo, you can go back and pick him up; you know where you left him. Honey, if you give him up, God can give you something better." Then I went home the following weekend. My godmother said, "Kesha, sometimes a person can love you and not be in love with you; there's a difference." That really sunk into my heart. I made up in my mind for sure that it was really time to let go of him. You see, even though we were not talking at this time, apart of me wanted to go back to him and a part of me didn't; I was hoping one day he would come back and realize it was me he was in love with and wanting to spend the rest of his life with. But then I realized that was never going to happen. The following weekend, I was at home watching a video tape called *I Got To Get Myself Together* by Bishop Noel Jones, and the things he was preaching about on that tape really sunk into my heart. It confirmed what my pastor was preaching about and the advice my godmother was giving me, such as, "Baby, you think you are giving up something when you come to God? No, you just about to get yourself something. If you let God choose for you, He knows what you like and what turns you on. If God chooses for you, he knows what He is doing, and then you won't be running here and there, trying to make the gift act right. Because if you choose for yourself; what you choose, it will have you up one day and over there the next day. You will be saying 'Nothing I do to please you seems to work.' You won't get tired of them; now you are sick of yourself. If you keep going back, God is going to put something so bad on that situation that you won't go back."

All of this just opened my eyes. I began to talk to God, and I realized this other woman he was with loves him too. She had been waiting all these many years for him to straighten up, and he still hasn't. It made me think about her feelings as well as mine. *She will be devastated,* I thought to myself. I decided the best thing for me to do was to walk away . I have learned that God really knows what's best for us, and God won't give you someone that will keep you depressed, up crying all night, running around with different women, and up pacing the floor all night, going around in circles and not knowing where to go or what to do.

Chapter Five:
The God of the Valley

But God wants his people to know that He is the God of the valley. When we are in the valley, he will deliver us out of every test, trial, and storm that occurs in our lives. You have to know that every situation comes into your life to make you stronger and bring you closer to God. He tells us in His word, Psalm 34:19, "Many are the afflictions of the righteous, but the Lord delivereth him out of them all." This lets one know that God will deliver us out of every storm, test, trial, oppression, and depression . It lets us know God will heal us and bring us through all things. In the midst of the valley, sometimes friends and family are few, the bills are due, and money is low, but just know that God is right there, carrying you. One thing we have got to know and remember is that God will never leave us nor forsake us. In the midst of being lied on, talked about, used, abused, and mistreated, you need to know that it is all working for your good. And if you hold on and keep praying and press your way to Jesus, He will heal you, and it will produce His glory and anointing in your life. All it takes is repenting to God and having a made up mind. After making up your mind, you should remove yourself from sin, confess it to God and ask Him to help you. Take it one day at a time. This is a daily walk, and if you begin to feel the urge to go back, just go down on your knees and pray. If necessary, you may even call on a spiritual Christian to help pray you through your situation. The Lord teaches us in His word to bear ye one another's burdens. (Gal.6:2) through all I have experienced, God has taught me to forgive and to love people from a pure heart. I pray this book has been a blessing to you God has inspired me to write this book in two volumes, so stay tuned for volume two, *Push Past The Pain.*

Reflections and Thoughts

Reflections and Thoughts

Reflections and Thoughts

Evangelist Lekeshia Bonner is the founder and director of Miracle Resource Center in Selma, Alabama. God has called her there in order to spiritually, emotionally, and physically empower and inspire the people of God through love, support, and prayer with the written word of God. She holds a certificate in ministerial training from Christian Life School Of Ministry, and she also holds a diploma in ministerial study from New Life Bible College.

www.ingramcontent.com/pod-product-compliance
Lightning Source LLC
Chambersburg PA
CBHW061229280526
45784CB00006B/2696